every day MATTERS

2018 DIARY

A YEAR OF INSPIRATION FOR THE MIND, BODY & SPIRIT

Every Day Matters 2018 Diary

First published in UK and USA in 2017 by
Watkins, an imprint of Watkins Media Limited
19 Cecil Court, London WC2N 4EZ
enquiries@watkinspublishing.co.uk

Designed by Watkins Media Limited

Author/Illustrator: Dani DiPirro
Art Direction/Design: Georgina Hewitt
Commissioning Editor: Kelly Thompson
Managing Editor: Fiona Robertson
Editor: Judy Barratt

Desk Diary ISBN: 978-1-78678-039-3
Pocket Diary ISBN: 978-1-78678-040-9

Colour reproduction by XY Digital, UK
Printed in China

Phases of the Moon:
- ● New moon
- ☽ First quarter
- ○ Full moon
- ☾ Last quarter

Signs of the Zodiac:

♒	Aquarius	January 20–February 17
♓	Pisces	February 18–March 19
♈	Aries	March 20–April 19
♉	Taurus	April 20–May 20
♊	Gemini	May 21–June 20
♋	Cancer	June 21–July 21
♌	Leo	July 22–August 22
♍	Virgo	August 23–September 22
♎	Libra	September 23–October 22
♏	Scorpio	October 23–November 21
♐	Sagittarius	November 22–December 20
♑	Capricorn	December 21–January 19

Abbreviations:
BCE: Before Common Era (equivalent of BC)
CE: Common Era (equivalent of AD)
UK: United Kingdom
SCO: Scotland
NIR: Northern Ireland
ROI: Republic of Ireland
CAN: Canada
USA: United States of America
NZ: New Zealand
AUS: Australia
ACT: Australian Capital Territory
NSW: New South Wales
NT: Northern Territory
QLD: Queensland
SA: South Australia
TAS: Tasmania
VIC: Victoria
WA: Western Australia

Publisher's Notes:
All dates relating to the zodiac signs and the phases of
the moon are based on Greenwich Mean Time (GMT).

All North American holiday dates are based on Eastern
Standard Time (EST).

Jewish and Islamic holidays begin at sundown on the
date given. Islamic holidays may vary by a day or two, as
the Islamic calendar is based on a combination of actual
sightings of the moon and astronomical calculations.

Note on Public Holidays:
Holiday dates were correct at the time of going to press.

2017

JANUARY

M	TU	W	TH	F	SA	SU
						1
2	3	4	5	6	7	8
9	10	11	12	13	14	15
16	17	18	19	20	21	22
23	24	25	26	27	28	29
30	31					

FEBRUARY

M	TU	W	TH	F	SA	SU
		1	2	3	4	5
6	7	8	9	10	11	12
13	14	15	16	17	18	19
20	21	22	23	24	25	26
27	28					

MARCH

M	TU	W	TH	F	SA	SU
		1	2	3	4	5
6	7	8	9	10	11	12
13	14	15	16	17	18	19
20	21	22	23	24	25	26
27	28	29	30	31		

APRIL

M	TU	W	TH	F	SA	SU
					1	2
3	4	5	6	7	8	9
10	11	12	13	14	15	16
17	18	19	20	21	22	23
24	25	26	27	28	29	30

MAY

M	TU	W	TH	F	SA	SU
1	2	3	4	5	6	7
8	9	10	11	12	13	14
15	16	17	18	19	20	21
22	23	24	25	26	27	28
29	30	31				

JUNE

M	TU	W	TH	F	SA	SU
			1	2	3	4
5	6	7	8	9	10	11
12	13	14	15	16	17	18
19	20	21	22	23	24	25
26	27	28	29	30		

JULY

M	TU	W	TH	F	SA	SU
					1	2
3	4	5	6	7	8	9
10	11	12	13	14	15	16
17	18	19	20	21	22	23
24	25	26	27	28	29	30
31						

AUGUST

M	TU	W	TH	F	SA	SU
	1	2	3	4	5	6
7	8	9	10	11	12	13
14	15	16	17	18	19	20
21	22	23	24	25	26	27
28	29	30	31			

SEPTEMBER

M	TU	W	TH	F	SA	SU
				1	2	3
4	5	6	7	8	9	10
11	12	13	14	15	16	17
18	19	20	21	22	23	24
25	26	27	28	29	30	

OCTOBER

M	TU	W	TH	F	SA	SU
						1
2	3	4	5	6	7	8
9	10	11	12	13	14	15
16	17	18	19	20	21	22
23	24	25	26	27	28	29
30	31					

NOVEMBER

M	TU	W	TH	F	SA	SU
		1	2	3	4	5
6	7	8	9	10	11	12
13	14	15	16	17	18	19
20	21	22	23	24	25	26
27	28	29	30			

DECEMBER

M	TU	W	TH	F	SA	SU
				1	2	3
4	5	6	7	8	9	10
11	12	13	14	15	16	17
18	19	20	21	22	23	24
25	26	27	28	29	30	31

2018

JANUARY

M	TU	W	TH	F	SA	SU
1	2	3	4	5	6	7
8	9	10	11	12	13	14
15	16	17	18	19	20	21
22	23	24	25	26	27	28
29	30	31				

FEBRUARY

M	TU	W	TH	F	SA	SU
			1	2	3	4
5	6	7	8	9	10	11
12	13	14	15	16	17	18
19	20	21	22	23	24	25
26	27	28				

MARCH

M	TU	W	TH	F	SA	SU
			1	2	3	4
5	6	7	8	9	10	11
12	13	14	15	16	17	18
19	20	21	22	23	24	25
26	27	28	29	30	31	

APRIL

M	TU	W	TH	F	SA	SU
						1
2	3	4	5	6	7	8
9	10	11	12	13	14	15
16	17	18	19	20	21	22
23	24	25	26	27	28	29
30						

MAY

M	TU	W	TH	F	SA	SU
	1	2	3	4	5	6
7	8	9	10	11	12	13
14	15	16	17	18	19	20
21	22	23	24	25	26	27
28	29	30	31			

JUNE

M	TU	W	TH	F	SA	SU
				1	2	3
4	5	6	7	8	9	10
11	12	13	14	15	16	17
18	19	20	21	22	23	24
25	26	27	28	29	30	

JULY

M	TU	W	TH	F	SA	SU
						1
2	3	4	5	6	7	8
9	10	11	12	13	14	15
16	17	18	19	20	21	22
23	24	25	26	27	28	29
30	31					

AUGUST

M	TU	W	TH	F	SA	SU
		1	2	3	4	5
6	7	8	9	10	11	12
13	14	15	16	17	18	19
20	21	22	23	24	25	26
27	28	29	30	31		

SEPTEMBER

M	TU	W	TH	F	SA	SU
					1	2
3	4	5	6	7	8	9
10	11	12	13	14	15	16
17	18	19	20	21	22	23
24	25	26	27	28	29	30

OCTOBER

M	TU	W	TH	F	SA	SU
1	2	3	4	5	6	7
8	9	10	11	12	13	14
15	16	17	18	19	20	21
22	23	24	25	26	27	28
29	30	31				

NOVEMBER

M	TU	W	TH	F	SA	SU
			1	2	3	4
5	6	7	8	9	10	11
12	13	14	15	16	17	18
19	20	21	22	23	24	25
26	27	28	29	30		

DECEMBER

M	TU	W	TH	F	SA	SU
					1	2
3	4	5	6	7	8	9
10	11	12	13	14	15	16
17	18	19	20	21	22	23
24	25	26	27	28	29	30
31						

2019

JANUARY

M	TU	W	TH	F	SA	SU
	1	2	3	4	5	6
7	8	9	10	11	12	13
14	15	16	17	18	19	20
21	22	23	24	25	26	27
28	29	30	31			

FEBRUARY

M	TU	W	TH	F	SA	SU
				1	2	3
4	5	6	7	8	9	10
11	12	13	14	15	16	17
18	19	20	21	22	23	24
25	26	27	28			

MARCH

M	TU	W	TH	F	SA	SU
				1	2	3
4	5	6	7	8	9	10
11	12	13	14	15	16	17
18	19	20	21	22	23	24
25	26	27	28	29	30	31

APRIL

M	TU	W	TH	F	SA	SU
1	2	3	4	5	6	7
8	9	10	11	12	13	14
15	16	17	18	19	20	21
22	23	24	25	26	27	28
29	30					

MAY

M	TU	W	TH	F	SA	SU
		1	2	3	4	5
6	7	8	9	10	11	12
13	14	15	16	17	18	19
20	21	22	23	24	25	26
27	28	29	30	31		

JUNE

M	TU	W	TH	F	SA	SU
					1	2
3	4	5	6	7	8	9
10	11	12	13	14	15	16
17	18	19	20	21	22	23
24	25	26	27	28	29	30

JULY

M	TU	W	TH	F	SA	SU
1	2	3	4	5	6	7
8	9	10	11	12	13	14
15	16	17	18	19	20	21
22	23	24	25	26	27	28
29	30	31				

AUGUST

M	TU	W	TH	F	SA	SU
			1	2	3	4
5	6	7	8	9	10	11
12	13	14	15	16	17	18
19	20	21	22	23	24	25
26	27	28	29	30	31	

SEPTEMBER

M	TU	W	TH	F	SA	SU
						1
2	3	4	5	6	7	8
9	10	11	12	13	14	15
16	17	18	19	20	21	22
23	24	25	26	27	28	29
30						

OCTOBER

M	TU	W	TH	F	SA	SU
	1	2	3	4	5	6
7	8	9	10	11	12	13
14	15	16	17	18	19	20
21	22	23	24	25	26	27
28	29	30	31			

NOVEMBER

M	TU	W	TH	F	SA	SU
				1	2	3
4	5	6	7	8	9	10
11	12	13	14	15	16	17
18	19	20	21	22	23	24
25	26	27	28	29	30	

DECEMBER

M	TU	W	TH	F	SA	SU
						1
2	3	4	5	6	7	8
9	10	11	12	13	14	15
16	17	18	19	20	21	22
23	24	25	26	27	28	29
30	31					

Argentina	Jan 1, Feb 12–13, Mar 24, Mar 30, Apr 2, May 1, May 25, Jun 17, Jun 20, Jul 9, Aug 20, Oct 8, Nov 26, Dec 8, Dec 25
Australia	Jan 1, Jan 26, Mar 5 (WA), Mar 12 (ACT, SA, TAS, VIC), Mar 30, March 31 (exc TAS, WA), Apr 2, Apr 25, May 7 (NT, QLD), Jun 4 (WA), Jun 11 (exc QLD, WA), Aug 6 (NSW, NT), Sep 24 (ACT, WA), Oct 1 (ACT, NSW, QLD, SA, WA), Dec 25–26
Austria	Jan 1, Jan 6, Apr 2, May 1, May 10, May 21, May 31, Aug 15, Oct 26, Nov 1, Dec 8, Dec 25–26
Belgium	Jan 1, Apr 1–2, May 1, May 10, May 20–21, Jul 21, Aug 15, Nov 1, Nov 11, Dec 25
Brazil	Jan 1, Mar 30, Apr 21, May 1, Sep 7, Oct 12, Nov 2, Nov 15, Dec 25
Canada	Jan 1, Mar 30, May 21, Jul 1–2, Sep 3, Oct 8, Nov 11–12, Dec 25
China	Jan 1, Feb 15–17, Apr 5, May 1, Jun 18, Sep 24, Oct 1–3
Denmark	Jan 1, Mar 29–30, Apr 1–2, Apr 27, May 10, May 20–21, Dec 25–26
Finland	Jan 1, Jan 6, Mar 30–Apr 2, May 1, May 10, May 20, Jun 23, Nov 3, Dec 6, Dec 25–26
France	Jan 1, Apr 2, May 1, May 8, May 10, May 21, Jul 14, Aug 15, Nov 1, Nov 11, Dec 25
Germany	Jan 1, Apr 2, May 1, May 10, May 21, Oct 3, Dec 25–26
Greece	Jan 1, Jan 6, Feb 19, Mar 25, Apr 6, Apr 8–9, May 1, May 28, Aug 15, Oct 28, Dec 25–26
India	Jan 26, Apr 9, Aug 15, Sep 29, Oct 2, Dec 25
Indonesia	Jan 1, Feb 16, Mar 17, Mar 30, Apr 13, May 1, May 10, May 29, Jun 15–16, Aug 17, Aug 22, Sep 11, Nov 20, Dec 25
Israel	Mar 1–2, Mar 26, Mar 31, Apr 6, Apr 19, May 13, May 20, Sep 10–11, Sep 19, Sep 24, Oct 1
Italy	Jan 1, Jan 6, Apr 1–2, Apr 25, May 1, Jun 2, Aug 15, Nov 1, Dec 8, Dec 25–26

Japan	Jan 1, Jan 8, Feb 11–12, Mar 21, Apr 29–30, May 3–5, Jul 16, Aug 11, Sep 17, Sep 23–24, Oct 8, Nov 3, Nov 23, Dec 23–24
Luxembourg	Jan 1, Apr 2, May 1, May 10, May 21, Jun 23, Aug 15, Nov 1, Dec 25–26
Mexico	Jan 1, Feb 5, Mar 19, Mar 21, May 1, Jul 1, Sep 16, Nov 19–20, Dec 1, Dec 25
Netherlands	Jan 1, Apr 1–2, Apr 27, May 10, May 20–21, Dec 25–26
New Zealand	Jan 1–2, Feb 6, Mar 30, Apr 2, Apr 25, Jun 4, Oct 22, Dec 25–26
Nigeria	Jan 1, Mar 30, Apr 2, May 1, May 29, Jun 15–16, Aug 22–23, Oct 1, Nov 21, Dec 25–26
Pakistan	Feb 5, Mar 23, May 1, Jun 15, Aug 14, Aug 22–23, Sep 12–13, Nov 21, Dec 25
Poland	Jan 1, Jan 6, Apr 1–2, May 1, May 3, May 20, May 31, Aug 15, Nov 1, Nov 11, Dec 25–26
Portugal	Jan 1, Mar 30, Apr 1, Apr 25, May 1, May 31, Jun 10, Aug 15, Oct 5, Nov 1, Dec 1, Dec 8, Dec 25
Republic of Ireland	Jan 1, Mar 17, Apr 2, May 7, Jun 4, Aug 6, Oct 29, Dec 25–26
Russia	Jan 1–4, Jan 7–8, Feb 23, Mar 8, Apr 30, May 1, May 9, Jun 11–12, Nov 4–5
South Africa	Jan 1, Mar 21, Mar 30, Apr 2, Apr 27, May 1, Jun 16, Aug 9, Sep 24, Dec 16–17, Dec 25–26
Spain	Jan 1, Jan 6, Mar 30, May 1, Aug 15, Oct 12, Nov 1, Dec 6, Dec 8, Dec 25
Sweden	Jan 1, Jan 6, Mar 30, Apr 1–2, May 1, May 10, May 20, Jun 6, Jun 23, Nov 3, Dec 24–26
Turkey	Jan 1, Apr 23, May 1, May 19, Aug 30, Oct 29
United Kingdom	Jan 1, Mar 30, Apr 2, May 7, May 28, Aug 27 (exc sco), Dec 25–26
United States	Jan 1, Jan 15, Feb 19, May 28, Jul 4, Sep 3, Oct 8, Nov 11, Nov 22, Dec 25

HAPPY 2018!

It's a new year — the perfect time to re-evaluate how to really make the most of your days. Ahead lie 12 months packed full of opportunities for learning, inspiration and new experiences with the potential to transform your life in the way you want.

Each month in this diary explores an inspirational theme specially chosen by positivity guide Dani DiPirro: Openness, Imagination, Awareness, Gratitude, Passion, Perspective, Friendship, Patience, Connection, Focus, Compassion and Transformation. For each month, Dani presents you with an affirmation that captures the essence of the theme, plus a set of weekly activities which, alongside thought-provoking quotations, will encourage you to grow in self-awareness and confidence, develop existing talents and find amazing new ones, too. With this diary as your companion, 2018 is set to be your most positive and successful year yet!

JANUARY

OPENNESS

2018 has arrived! Now is the time to consciously open your heart and mind to all the potential this year has to offer – whether you are looking for new opportunities in your career, your relationships, your self-image or any other aspect of your life. Being open-hearted is the first step on a journey to explore alternative ways of thinking and being, make new connections and live with more joy. Openness makes us more resilient, too; when we're open, we whole-heartedly embrace change instead of just accepting it. Openness breeds more honesty in ourselves and others, strengthening bonds and helping us make better, smarter decisions. It gives our thoughts and emotions more space to move, change shape and cause delight, like bubbles floating on the breeze. This month, open the windows of your heart and mind, and let some fresh air into your life.

AFFIRMATION OF THE MONTH

I open my mind to new ways of growing.

JANUARY 1 – JANUARY 7

openness

1 / MONDAY

New Year's Day
Kwanzaa ends

2 / TUESDAY ○

Public holiday (SCO, NZ)

3 / WEDNESDAY

NOTES

JOHN BARRYMORE (1882–1942), AMERICAN ACTOR

4 / THURSDAY

5 / FRIDAY

6 / SATURDAY

Epiphany

7 / SUNDAY

Christmas Day (Orthodox)

LET HAPPINESS FIND YOU

It's human nature to seek happiness, but we also need to be ready to receive it unexpectedly. Make a list of five feel-good surprises from last year — a visit from an old friend; a chance conversation that led to a new adventure; a gift that arrived out of the blue … Then begin each day this week ready to let happiness sneak in to find you, and embrace it fully when it does.

JANUARY 8 – JANUARY 14

openness

8 / MONDAY ☾

9 / TUESDAY

10 / WEDNESDAY

NOTES

11 / THURSDAY

12 / FRIDAY

13 / SATURDAY

14 / SUNDAY

New Year's Day (Orthodox)

SHARE YOUR DREAMS

We often worry that others will judge our ambitions as fanciful, but opening up about our dreams is often the first step to making them real. This week, identify one ambition you have for the year and share it with a trusted friend. Ask for support and advice to help you make your dream a reality.

openness

15 / MONDAY

Martin Luther King, Jr Day

16 / TUESDAY

17 / WEDNESDAY ●

NOTES

"Seeking means: to have a goal; but finding means: to be free, to be receptive, to have no goal."
HERMANN HESSE (1877–1962), GERMAN-BORN SWISS AUTHOR

18 / THURSDAY

19 / FRIDAY

20 / SATURDAY

21 / SUNDAY

TAKE YOUR EYE OFF THE PRIZE

Although focus is essential to achieving goals, developing results-oriented "tunnel vision" can stop us savouring the moment and blind us to unexpected opportunities. Every day this week, spend some time consciously letting go of your striving and focus on being in the present, opening yourself up to the rich reality that surrounds you.

JANUARY 22 – JANUARY 28

openness

22 / MONDAY

23 / TUESDAY

24 / WEDNESDAY ☽

NOTES

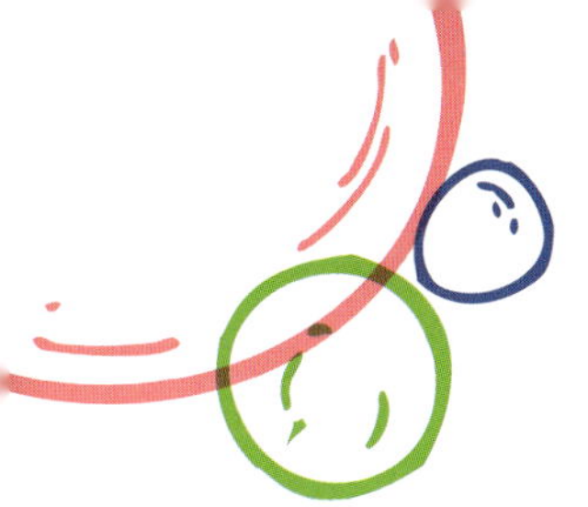

GEORGE BERNARD SHAW (1856–1950), IRISH PLAYWRIGHT

25 / THURSDAY

Burns Night

26 / FRIDAY

Australia Day

27 / SATURDAY

International Holocaust
Remembrance Day

28 / SUNDAY

BE OPEN TO DIFFERENT PERSPECTIVES

Holding a firm belief shows great strength of character — but only if we approach alternative viewpoints with respect and openness. This week, choose a belief you hold dear and spend some time investigating the opposite point of view. In doing this, your only intention is to be open to the information and ideas you find, even if you disagree with them.

JANUARY OVERVIEW

M	TU	W	TH	F	SA	SU
1	2	3	4	5	6	7
8	9	10	11	12	13	14
15	16	17	18	19	20	21
22	23	24	25	26	27	28
29	30	31	1	2	3	4

This month I am grateful for …

Reflections on OPENNESS

In what ways did you open your heart and mind this month?

What benefits did you gain from being more open and receptive this month?

In what ways will you continue to value openness during the rest of the year?

FEBRUARY

IMAGINATION

Imagination is one of our most precious resources, helping us find a way forward if we feel bogged down by routine, glimpse better ways of being and gain more insight into the mysteries of life, love and the universe. Children are naturally creative in their exploration of the world around them, but as we get older we become more inclined to rely on what we already know and on logic, facts and figures, rather than opening our minds to what we might imagine. This pragmatic approach does not always feel fulfilling and often an imaginative leap in the dark is what's needed. In the coming weeks we'll be looking at ways to put logic to one side and reconnect with imagination, tapping in to the innate creativity we all have. Look below the surface of what you know to be true and uncover the dreams, the silly, the magical and the mindblowing!

AFFIRMATION OF THE MONTH
I set my imagination free.

JANUARY 29 – FEBRUARY 4

imagination

29 / MONDAY	30 / TUESDAY	31 / WEDNESDAY ○

NOTES

1 / THURSDAY

St Brigid's Day (Imbolc)
Black History Month begins
(CAN, USA)

2 / FRIDAY

Candlemas
Groundhog Day

3 / SATURDAY

4 / SUNDAY

RELEASE YOUR IMAGINATION

Caught up in humdrum daily tasks, we often forget to use our imagination. This week, find 30 minutes to doodle pictures inspired by your inner creativity. Perhaps you will draw scenes from strange worlds, or mythical beasts, or intricate patterns or symbols … Look at your drawings closely. What is your imagination telling you?

imagination

5 / MONDAY

6 / TUESDAY

Waitangi Day

7 / WEDNESDAY ☾

NOTES

"You can't depend on your eyes when your imagination is out of focus."

MARK TWAIN (1835–1910), AMERICAN AUTHOR

8 / THURSDAY

9 / FRIDAY

10 / SATURDAY

11 / SUNDAY

GO BEYOND WHAT YOU KNOW

This week, suspend rationality and turn to your imagination for explanations of the world around you. Why is the sky blue? Why do clouds move? Why do people walk upright? Every morning, kick-start your creativity with a question like this and see what your imagination comes up with.

FEBRUARY 12 – FEBRUARY 18

12 / MONDAY

Abraham Lincoln's birthday

13 / TUESDAY

Shrove Tuesday

14 / WEDNESDAY

St Valentine's Day
Ash Wednesday

NOTES

15 / THURSDAY ●

Nirvana Day

16 / FRIDAY

Chinese New Year
(Year of the Dog)
Losar (Tibetan New Year)

17 / SATURDAY

18 / SUNDAY ♓

IMAGINE THE YEAR INTO BEING

Imagine, this week, some of the key experiences you'd love to have this year (keep them realistic, even if hard to achieve), and choose a single word to represent each one. Write all the words on a piece of paper in big, colourful letters, frame it and hang it on the wall to inspire you every day.

19 / MONDAY

Presidents' Day

20 / TUESDAY

21 / WEDNESDAY

NOTES

LEWIS CARROLL (1832–1898), ENGLISH AUTHOR

22 / THURSDAY

23 / FRIDAY ☽

24 / SATURDAY

25 / SUNDAY

PLAY ALL DAY

To prevent lacklustre routines from taking the colour out of life, try taking an off-the-wall approach to mundane tasks. While you clean the bathroom this week, make up a rhyme; while you fold the laundry, sing a song; while you write a to-do list, use coloured pens and curly writing. The sillier the better when it comes to tackling routine activities over the next seven days.

FEBRUARY OVERVIEW

M	TU	W	TH	F	SA	SU
29	30	31	1	2	3	4
5	6	7	8	9	10	11
12	13	14	15	16	17	18
19	20	21	22	23	24	25
26	27	28	1	2	3	4

This month I am grateful for . . .

Reflections on IMAGINATION

How did you choose to tap into your imagination this month?

In what ways did you view everyday life differently or with more wonder?

In the future, how can you continue to connect with your imagination?

MARCH

AWARENESS

When we pay attention to what is going on around us and within us, we are awake and can appreciate each moment as it happens, instead of constantly mulling over the past or worrying about the future. There is always more to understand than meets the eye, so we need to allow ourselves to go deep into our experience of the present, instead of seeing only the tip of the iceberg. This month is all about tuning in more closely to the moment, giving ourselves more openings for insight, compassion and joy. And the more aware we are of what we experience, the more conscious we'll be of our own responses. This increased self-awareness brings with it a powerful opportunity to take something positive away from every encounter, every relationship and every situation. This month is the month to live fully aware.

AFFIRMATION OF THE MONTH

I am open to the detail of every moment.

26 / MONDAY

27 / TUESDAY

28 / WEDNESDAY

Purim begins at sundown

NOTES

1 / THURSDAY

St David's Day
World Book Day

2 / FRIDAY ○

Holi (Festival of Colours)

3 / SATURDAY

4 / SUNDAY

SWITCH OFF THE AUTO-PILOT

Rushing through habitual tasks, it's easy to miss the enchanting details of life. This week, take note of ten things you've stopped noticing about a journey you make every day. Perhaps you'll be struck by signs of the season, or the colours of flowers, or decorative details of the houses you pass, or something else surprising …

MARCH 5 – MARCH 11

awareness

5 / MONDAY

Labour Day (WA)

6 / TUESDAY

7 / WEDNESDAY

NOTES

> "The ultimate value of life depends upon awareness . . . rather than upon mere survival."
>
> ARISTOTLE (*c.* 384–322BCE), ANCIENT GREEK PHILOSOPHER

8 / THURSDAY

International Women's Day

9 / FRIDAY ☾

10 / SATURDAY

11 / SUNDAY

Daylight Saving Time starts
(CAN, USA)
Mother's Day (UK)

MARCH 12 – MARCH 18

awareness

12 / MONDAY

Commonwealth Day
Public holiday (ACT, SA,
TAS, VIC)

13 / TUESDAY

14 / WEDNESDAY

NOTES

15 / THURSDAY

16 / FRIDAY

17 / SATURDAY ●

St Patrick's Day

18 / SUNDAY

SEEK OUT NEW SENSORY EXPERIENCES

Last week you used your senses to expand your awareness; this week, build on that and actively create fresh sensory experiences. Every day, try a food or type of music that's new to you, or find a new view to appreciate, or feel an unfamiliar fabric on your skin. As you experience them, allow the sensations to fill your awareness.

19 / MONDAY

20 / TUESDAY ♈

Spring Equinox (UK, ROI, CAN, USA)
Autumn Equinox (AUS, NZ)

21 / WEDNESDAY

NOTES

22 / THURSDAY

23 / FRIDAY

24 / SATURDAY

25 / SUNDAY

British Summer Time begins
Palm Sunday

FOCUS ON THE PRESENT

To be aware, we need to really inhabit the current moment. This week, carry paper and a pen with you. When you become preoccupied with the past or future, spend five to ten minutes journalling about what's happening right now, in the present. Note details, such as the weather, how you're breathing or how you're feeling, to bring yourself back to the now.

MARCH 26 – APRIL 1

26 / MONDAY

27 / TUESDAY

28 / WEDNESDAY

NOTES

> *"Even a little effort toward spiritual awareness will protect you from the greatest fear."*
>
> VEDA VYASA, LEGENDARY INDIAN AUTHOR OF THE *BHAGAVAD GITA*

29 / THURSDAY

Maundy Thursday

30 / FRIDAY

Good Friday
Pesach (Passover) begins
at sundown

31 / SATURDAY ○

Easter Saturday

1 / SUNDAY

Easter Sunday
April Fools' Day

CONNECT WITH YOUR INNER STRENGTH

What would you love to do, but don't dare to try? Turn your awareness within and listen for the voice that tells you you can do it. This is the voice of your inner strength. When you become aware of it, write down its positive message on a piece of paper to carry with you and inspire you as you make your dream a reality.

MARCH OVERVIEW

M	TU	W	TH	F	SA	SU
26	27	28	1	2	3	4
5	6	7	8	9	10	11
12	13	14	15	16	17	18
19	20	21	22	23	24	25
26	27	28	29	30	31	1

This month I am grateful for . . .

Reflections on AWARENESS

In what ways did you choose to be more aware this month?

What does the word "awareness" now mean to you?

How will you strive to be more self-aware in the future?

APRIL

GRATITUDE

Cultivating gratitude is the best way to start living positively. Research has shown gratitude can make us happier, less stressed, less prone to negative emotions such as envy, physically healthier, more likeable and even more successful. Try imagining your life as a garden, and strive to be thankful for each and every sign of life. Remember: what some view as a weed, like the lowly dandelion, others see as a beautiful opportunity to make a wish. Every obstacle we encounter in life has something to teach us, if we can only be open to its message. If we are grateful for what we have now, we stop striving for a "better" future or longing for a halcyon past. Instead, we allow the present to fulfil us. This month, look for all you have to be grateful for.

AFFIRMATION OF THE MONTH

I am grateful for all that surrounds me.

APRIL 2 – APRIL 8

gratitude

2 / MONDAY

Easter Monday

3 / TUESDAY

4 / WEDNESDAY

NOTES

5 / THURSDAY

6 / FRIDAY

7 / SATURDAY

Pesach (Passover) ends
at sundown

8 / SUNDAY ☾

Easter (Orthodox)

CONNECT WITH YOUR JOY

The experience of joy is itself a kind of thankfulness. When you allow yourself to feel freely joyful about something, you give a thank-you note to the universe. Nurture gratitude this week by identifying at least one small but special activity that brings you true joy and make time for it each day.

APRIL 9 – APRIL 15

gratitude

9 / MONDAY

10 / TUESDAY

11 / WEDNESDAY

NOTES

12 / THURSDAY

13 / FRIDAY

14 / SATURDAY

15 / SUNDAY

BE GRATEFUL FOR MISTAKES

Spend some time reflecting on and writing about a mistake you've made in the past that, in fact, led to a better-than-expected outcome or somehow saved you from harm. To channel your inner wisdom, use a free-writing technique: write whatever comes to your mind without stopping for at least five minutes.

gratitude

16 / MONDAY ●

17 / TUESDAY

18 / WEDNESDAY

NOTES

19 / THURSDAY

20 / FRIDAY ♉

21 / SATURDAY

22 / SUNDAY ☽

Earth Day

MAKE A LUCK LIST

This week, recognize your own good luck. Make a list of at least ten things you feel fortunate to have – from friends to family to a fulfilling job. Then, if possible, write thank-you notes to the people responsible. (There's no need to actually send them if you'd prefer not to.)

gratitude

23 / MONDAY

St George's Day

24 / TUESDAY

25 / WEDNESDAY

Anzac Day

NOTES

26 / THURSDAY

27 / FRIDAY

28 / SATURDAY

29 / SUNDAY

REFLECT ON YOUR ROOTS

A sense of gratitude can help us cope with many things in life, including the pain of loss. In honour of those you have lost and also of more distant ancestors, find out what you can about your heritage, perhaps by asking other relatives or by doing some online digging. You could draw up a family tree to express your gratitude toward those who have helped shape your life.

APRIL OVERVIEW

M	TU	W	TH	F	SA	SU
26	27	28	29	30	31	1
2	3	4	5	6	7	8
9	10	11	12	13	14	15
16	17	18	19	20	21	22
23	24	25	26	27	28	29
30	1	2	3	4	5	6

This month I am grateful for . . .

Reflections on GRATITUDE

What did you learn about gratitude this month?

How did you best express thankfulness in recent weeks?

In the future, what can you do to make gratitude part of your everyday life?

MAY

PASSION

Passion shows itself in myriad ways – the heartfelt debate on a subject you feel strongly about, the complete absorption in a hobby you love, the heat that burns in a kiss. Like palm trees spreading their vibrant leaves upward and outward across the sky, true passion reaches farther than we may have thought possible, its commanding energy driving us to accomplish our goals. Our passions bring us together – think of the instant connection sparked between people who share a deep enthusiasm for the same thing, or the hunger we experience to be with certain people – and all the more so if we are willing to share our profound desires with others. This month is all about discovering what your truest passions are and aiming high to fulfil them. Hold on tight – May is going to exceed your wildest expectations!

AFFIRMATION OF THE MONTH

I let passion into my soul.

APRIL 30 — MAY 6

passion

30 / MONDAY ○

1 / TUESDAY

Beltane
May Day

2 / WEDNESDAY

NOTES

3 / THURSDAY

4 / FRIDAY

5 / SATURDAY

Cinco de Mayo

6 / SUNDAY

RECONNECT WITH YOUR PASSION

Do you remember an all-absorbing passion you felt as a child? This week, schedule time to recapture it. If you loved horses, book a one-off riding lesson. If it was soccer, lose yourself in a kickabout. Did you love to sing? Download your favourite song and belt it out! Then consider if you want to make this a bigger part of your life.

passion

7 / MONDAY

Early May Bank Holiday
(UK, ROI)
May Day (NT, QLD)

8 / TUESDAY ☾

9 / WEDNESDAY

NOTES

JEAN-PAUL SARTRE (1905–1980), FRENCH PHILOSOPHER AND AUTHOR

10 / THURSDAY

Ascension Day

11 / FRIDAY

12 / SATURDAY

13 / SUNDAY

Mother's Day (CAN, USA, AUS, NZ)

LET PASSION SEIZE YOU

This week, explore potential new enthusiasms. Every day, try out one activity that you've never done before but could become your next big thing. It could be a language-learning app or an exercise class, or perhaps gardening, painting or woodwork … whatever appeals. Keep exploring until you find what sets your passion alight.

MAY 14 – MAY 20

passion

14 / MONDAY

15 / TUESDAY ●

Ramadan begins at sundown

16 / WEDNESDAY

NOTES

GIACOMO CASANOVA (1725–1798), ITALIAN ADVENTURER AND AUTHOR

17 / THURSDAY

18 / FRIDAY

19 / SATURDAY

20 / SUNDAY

Pentecost (Whit Sunday)

INFLAME OTHERS WITH YOUR PASSION

Share your passion this week by showing others what you love to do most. If you adore nature, take a friend hiking; if you are passionate about writing, put your feelings down in a letter; if you are a movie nut, invite a friend along. Those you invite into your passion will appreciate your joy and enthusiasm as precious gifts.

MAY 21 – MAY 27
passion

21 / MONDAY ♊

Victoria Day (CAN, except NS, NU, QC)

22 / TUESDAY ☽

Buddha's birthday (in some countries)

23 / WEDNESDAY

NOTES

24 / THURSDAY

25 / FRIDAY

26 / SATURDAY

27 / SUNDAY

BREAK OUT OF A RUT

Does it ever feel like life has lost some of its joy? This week, focus on getting the adrenaline pumping again by shaking things up. Challenge your tastebuds with a new cuisine. Push yourself to the limit as you work out. Don't take your love life for granted; really focus on your partner and on what attracts you to each other.

28 / MONDAY

Spring Bank Holiday (UK)
Memorial Day (USA)

29 / TUESDAY ○

Vesak Day (Buddha Day)

30 / WEDNESDAY

NOTES

31 / THURSDAY

1 / FRIDAY

2 / SATURDAY

3 / SUNDAY

FIND YOUR WHITE HOT

When it comes to passion, the hotter it is, the better! This week, focus on what gets you especially excited. Is it a particular person or experience or thought? Every day, note down what raised your feelings to fever pitch. At the week's end, reflect on how you can have more of these moments when you feel truly alive.

MAY OVERVIEW

M	TU	W	TH	F	SA	SU
30	1	2	3	4	5	6
7	8	9	10	11	12	13
14	15	16	17	18	19	20
21	22	23	24	25	26	27
28	29	30	31	1	2	3

This month I am grateful for . . .

____

____

____

____

____

____

____

Reflections on PASSION

How did you focus on passion this month?

What does it mean for you to be passionate?

How can you connect more often with your innermost passions in future?

JUNE

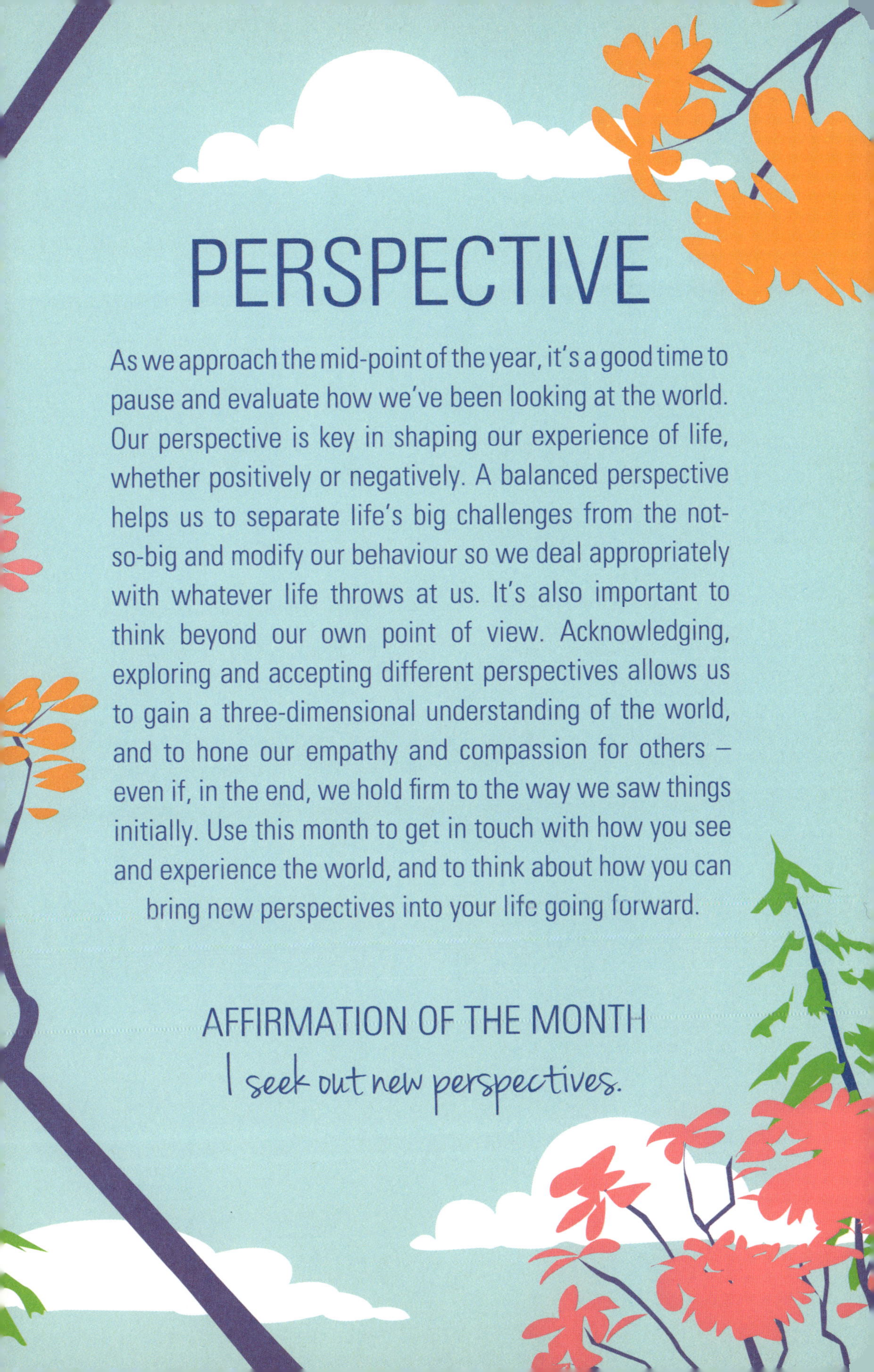

PERSPECTIVE

As we approach the mid-point of the year, it's a good time to pause and evaluate how we've been looking at the world. Our perspective is key in shaping our experience of life, whether positively or negatively. A balanced perspective helps us to separate life's big challenges from the not-so-big and modify our behaviour so we deal appropriately with whatever life throws at us. It's also important to think beyond our own point of view. Acknowledging, exploring and accepting different perspectives allows us to gain a three-dimensional understanding of the world, and to hone our empathy and compassion for others — even if, in the end, we hold firm to the way we saw things initially. Use this month to get in touch with how you see and experience the world, and to think about how you can bring new perspectives into your life going forward.

AFFIRMATION OF THE MONTH
I seek out new perspectives.

JUNE 4 – JUNE 10

perspective

4 / MONDAY

June Bank Holiday (ROI)
Queen's birthday celebrated
(NZ)
Western Australia Day (WA)

5 / TUESDAY

6 / WEDNESDAY ☾

NOTES

7 / THURSDAY

8 / FRIDAY

9 / SATURDAY

10 / SUNDAY

REVISIT THE PAST

The past has a powerful impact on the way you see the present, but what you remember is often shaped as much by your personal perspective as by facts. This week, meet a friend and recall a past event you both experienced, whether negative or positive. How do your accounts of the experience and your emotions differ? What does that tell you?

JUNE 11 – JUNE 17

perspective

11 / MONDAY

Queen's birthday celebrated
(AUS, except QLD, WA)

12 / TUESDAY

13 / WEDNESDAY ●

NOTES

FRANCES HODGSON BURNETT (1849–1924), ENGLISH-BORN NOVELIST

14 / THURSDAY

Ramadan ends at sundown
(Eid al-Fitr)

15 / FRIDAY

16 / SATURDAY

17 / SUNDAY

Father's Day (UK, ROI,
CAN, USA)

SEE CHALLENGES IN A NEW LIGHT

This week, use the perspective of a holistic metaphor to see any difficulties as simply part of life. Complete this sentence: "The whole world is a _______." Then, if "the whole world is a forest", the people you know might be the trees, your troubles the brambles and fallen logs, your emotions a rushing stream, and so on.

18 / MONDAY

19 / TUESDAY

20 / WEDNESDAY ☽

NOTES

21 / THURSDAY ♋

Summer Solstice (UK, ROI, CAN, USA)
Winter Solstice (AUS, NZ)

22 / FRIDAY

23 / SATURDAY

24 / SUNDAY

PINPOINT THE POSITIVE

At the start of the week, identify three thorny issues in your life — you might choose specific relationship or work concerns, or more abstract problems, such as lack of time. What can you learn from each problem? Patience? Tolerance? Time management? Tackle each worry in turn by taking a positive perspective on it.

25 / MONDAY

26 / TUESDAY

27 / WEDNESDAY

NOTES

"No two persons ever read the same book."
EDMUND WILSON (1895–1972), AMERICAN AUTHOR

28 / THURSDAY ○

29 / FRIDAY

30 / SATURDAY

1 / SUNDAY

Canada Day

EXCHANGE VIEWPOINTS

This week, focus on your perspective as just one of many valid opinions. Find a thought-provoking paragraph in Monday's news and spend ten minutes reflecting on what it means to you. Ask a friend to read the same piece and do the same. Discuss your thoughts, thinking about how the same words can inspire different ideas.

JUNE OVERVIEW

M	TU	W	TH	F	SA	SU
28	29	30	31	1	2	3
4	5	6	7	8	9	10
11	12	13	14	15	16	17
18	19	20	21	22	23	24
25	26	27	28	29	30	1

This month I am grateful for . . .

Reflections on PERSPECTIVE

How did you shift your perspective this month?

How does it feel to think about things from a different viewpoint?

How can you continually seek out fresh perspectives?

JULY

FRIENDSHIP

The bonds that our early ancestors formed were essential to humankind's survival, enabling them to build communities that protected and nourished. Like birds flying in formation, even today we humans still find strength in numbers, relying on one another for support and guidance. Friendship provides a means to care for others and to feel cared for; to trust and to feel trusted. It creates a space for joy and laughter and for making shared memories. It lifts us up when we're sad, gives us someone to celebrate our successes with and reminds us of all that's good and meaningful. Above all, friendship provides a sense of belonging, a connectedness that means there's always somewhere to turn. The activities this month offer a chance to develop empathy and compassion, and an opportunity to build and enjoy friendship in all its guises.

AFFIRMATION OF THE MONTH

I strive to be a good friend.

2 / MONDAY

Canada Day observed

3 / TUESDAY

4 / WEDNESDAY

Independence Day (USA)

NOTES

5 / THURSDAY

6 / FRIDAY ☾

7 / SATURDAY

8 / SUNDAY

BE GRATEFUL FOR YOUR FRIENDS

You are lucky indeed if you have even just one true friend who loves you just as you are. Celebrate that friendship this week by sending or emailing an appreciative thank-you note to let your friend know how grateful you are for your relationship. Be sure to say something specific about why you're thankful.

friendship

9 / MONDAY

10 / TUESDAY

11 / WEDNESDAY

NOTES

12 / THURSDAY

Orangemen's Day (NIR)

13 / FRIDAY ●

14 / SATURDAY

Bastille Day

15 / SUNDAY

HELP A FRIEND TO SHARE A TROUBLE

Sometimes even close friends fear burdening us with their woes. Strengthen your bond with a friend in need this week by reaching out to them and inviting them to open up about any troubles. Listen attentively, asking questions that encourage them to talk more if necessary.

16 / MONDAY

17 / TUESDAY

18 / WEDNESDAY

NOTES

19 / THURSDAY ☽

20 / FRIDAY

21 / SATURDAY

22 / SUNDAY ♌

CREATE A SUN OF FRIENDSHIP

In dark times friends can be real rays of light. This week, remind yourself how yours have helped you by thinking of a sad moment in your life. Draw a circle on a sheet of paper, then, emanating outward like rays of sunshine, write the names of all the friends who helped you get through that time, in big ways or small.

23 / MONDAY

24 / TUESDAY

25 / WEDNESDAY

NOTES

26 / THURSDAY   **27 / FRIDAY** ○   **28 / SATURDAY**

29 / SUNDAY

REACH OUT TO AN OLD FRIEND

Friendships can be hard to maintain. Some end for a reason, but others simply drift away. Reach out to an old friend who you miss this week via email, phone or social media. Open a dialogue that invites you both to share stories about how you remember each other. Then compare your friend's view with how you see yourself now.

JULY OVERVIEW

M	TU	W	TH	F	SA	SU
25	26	27	28	29	30	1
2	3	4	5	6	7	8
9	10	11	12	13	14	15
16	17	18	19	20	21	22
23	24	25	26	27	28	29
30	31	1	2	3	4	5

This month I am grateful for . . .

Reflections on FRIENDSHIP

How did it feel to focus on friendship this month?

How did you go about appreciating the friendships in your life?

In what ways will you celebrate friendship more in the future?

AUGUST

PATIENCE

Living mindfully, and enjoying each moment to the fullest, requires patience. Only by learning to inhabit the moment, without brushing aside our current experience as we hurry through our to-do lists, can we live in total appreciation of life's beauty. Instead of constantly striving to achieve everything in an instant, patience allows us to experience our days and weeks slowly unfolding, like a vine growing and unfurling little by little each day. And the good news is that patience is a skill we can learn, practise and improve. The activities in the weeks that follow encourage you to nurture your capacity for patience in order to bring a greater sense of calm and appreciation into your life. If being patient is typically a struggle for you, the exercises for this month will start you on a path to more relaxation and acceptance.

AFFIRMATION OF THE MONTH

I am patient in all things.

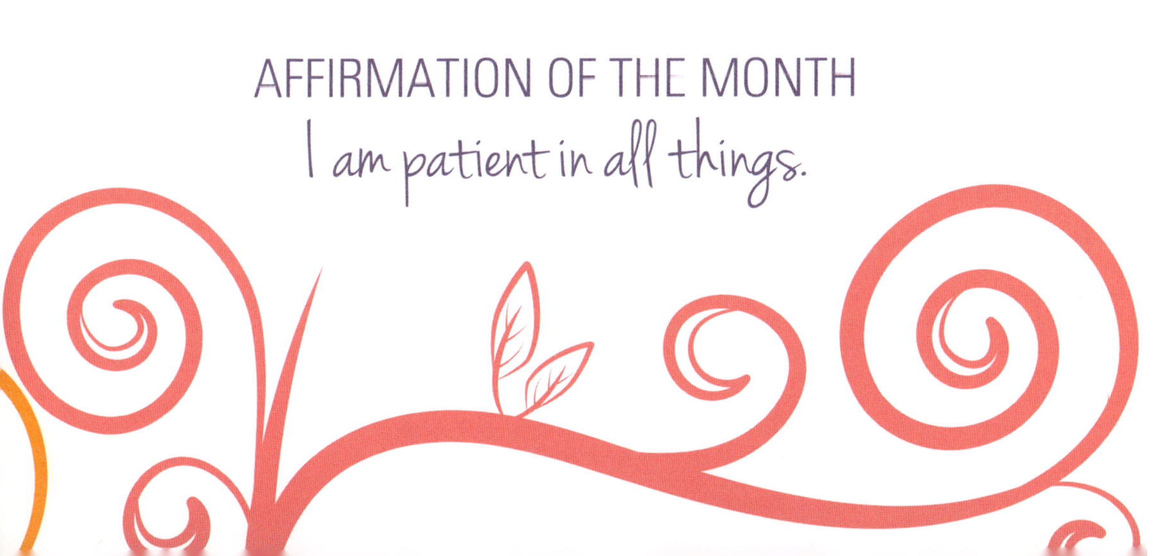

JULY 30 – AUGUST 5

patience

30 / MONDAY

31 / TUESDAY

1 / WEDNESDAY

Lughnasadh (Lammas)

NOTES

2 / THURSDAY

3 / FRIDAY

4 / SATURDAY ☾

5 / SUNDAY

GO SLOWLY

This week's challenge is to stop rushing so much. Instead, try to move slowly and mindfully through as many daily tasks as possible. Do one job at a time, drive at the speed limit, put your phone away when you're eating and chew each mouthful before swallowing. Pay attention to how it feels to go at this more measured pace.

AUGUST 6 – AUGUST 12
patience

6 / MONDAY

August Bank Holiday (ROI, SCO)
Public holiday (NSW, NT)

7 / TUESDAY

8 / WEDNESDAY

NOTES

9 / THURSDAY

10 / FRIDAY

11 / SATURDAY ●

12 / SUNDAY

GO EASY ON YOURSELF

This week, think of a task that is causing you frustration, such as an unfinished work report or DIY project. List all the reasons why you haven't done it yet, and plan how you can overcome each one. Can you use these findings to be more patient with yourself when other goals take longer to reach than expected?

AUGUST 13 – AUGUST 19

13 / MONDAY

14 / TUESDAY

15 / WEDNESDAY

NOTES

16 / THURSDAY

17 / FRIDAY

18 / SATURDAY ☽

19 / SUNDAY

MAKE TIME FOR THINKING

We live in a world of constant activity, and it's often tempting to leap into action to achieve our aims as soon as possible. This week, try to pause and reflect before you initiate any new projects. If you first allow a plan to unfurl fully in your mind, your actions will become more purposeful and more efficient in the long run.

AUGUST 20 – AUGUST 26

patience

20 / MONDAY

21 / TUESDAY

Eid al-Adha (Feast of the Sacrifice) begins at sundown

22 / WEDNESDAY

NOTES

FRANKLIN D. ROOSEVELT (1882–1945), AMERICAN PRESIDENT

23 / THURSDAY ♍

24 / FRIDAY

25 / SATURDAY

26 / SUNDAY ○

ENJOY ANTICIPATION

Sometimes we have to wait for beauty to reveal itself. This week, go to your local flower store and buy a single, closed bud. Put it in water and take a photo of it every day until it has opened fully. Enjoy the slow process of beauty's blossoming. The sequence of photos will act as a reminder of the fruits of patience.

AUGUST 27 – SEPTEMBER 2

patience

27 / MONDAY

Summer Bank Holiday (UK, except SCO)

28 / TUESDAY

29 / WEDNESDAY

NOTES

30 / THURSDAY

31 / FRIDAY

1 / SATURDAY

2 / SUNDAY

Father's Day (AUS, NZ)

CELEBRATE OVERCOMING A CHALLENGE

Only by facing difficulty can we learn what we are truly capable of. This week, think of a major challenge you've encountered this year. Spend 15 minutes writing down all the positive things you learned about yourself during this time. Can any of these points help you be more patient with yourself during a current challenge?

AUGUST OVERVIEW

M	TU	W	TH	F	SA	SU
30	31	1	2	3	4	5
6	7	8	9	10	11	12
13	14	15	16	17	18	19
20	21	22	23	24	25	26
27	28	29	30	31	1	2

This month I am grateful for . . .

Reflections on PATIENCE

How did you practise being more patient this month?

What tangible benefits did you experience as a result of being more patient?

In what ways will you look to practise patience more often in the future?

SEPTEMBER

CONNECTION

Like the strands of a spider's web, our lives are intricately connected with the lives of the people around us, whether we know them or not. We are all linked through the information, ideas, thoughts and beliefs we gather from the world, and all these connections have the potential to strengthen or transform us if we keep our hearts and minds open. September is your month to focus on connecting – and on reconnecting – whether that's with new or existing social or work contacts, with an old friend or with a setting that used to be special to you. The weekly exercises will help you consider how the people and places you are currently linked to make you feel, and how you can make the most of relationships both new and old. In this way you'll gain a deeper, richer understanding of yourself, others and the world around you.

AFFIRMATION OF THE MONTH

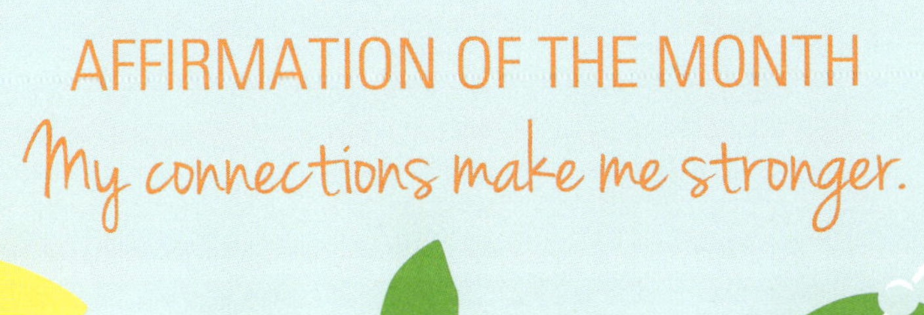

connection

3 / MONDAY ☾

Labor Day (CAN, USA)

4 / TUESDAY

5 / WEDNESDAY

NOTES

SUSAN SONTAG (1933–2004), AMERICAN AUTHOR

6 / THURSDAY

7 / FRIDAY

8 / SATURDAY

9 / SUNDAY ●

Rosh Hashanah (Jewish New Year) begins at sundown

LISTEN CLOSELY TO SOMEONE

Connection starts with paying attention. This week, identify someone you don't know well but see often (perhaps a colleague at work or another parent at school). Start a conversation, listening closely to what he or she has to say. Be enthusiastic and keep your body language open. See where this connection takes you.

10 / MONDAY

Islamic New Year (first day of
Muharram) begins at sundown

11 / TUESDAY

12 / WEDNESDAY

NOTES

13 / THURSDAY

14 / FRIDAY

15 / SATURDAY

16 / SUNDAY

CREATE A WEB OF LIFE

Write your name on a piece of paper, then add the names of family, friends and colleagues, linking them to each other and to you. Continue adding names until you have drawn a web that maps your life and the people in it. Spend some time considering how your actions and interactions vibrate through this web.

connection

17 / MONDAY ☽

18 / TUESDAY

Yom Kippur (Day of Atonement)
begins at sundown

19 / WEDNESDAY

NOTES

20 / THURSDAY

21 / FRIDAY

International Day of Peace

22 / SATURDAY

23 / SUNDAY ♎

Autumn Equinox (UK, ROI, CAN, USA)
Spring Equinox (AUS, NZ)
Sukkot (Feast of the Tabernacles) begins at sundown

DEEPEN A RELATIONSHIP

This week, create a stronger connection with a loved one by scheduling time to spend together to discuss questions such as these: *What matters most to you in life? What is the best decision you've ever made? What is the worst decision? What do you want to achieve in the next 12 months?* Listen closely to each other.

connection

24 / MONDAY

Public holiday (ACT, WA)

25 / TUESDAY ○

26 / WEDNESDAY

NOTES

"When one tugs at a single thing in nature,
he finds it attached to the rest of the world."

JOHN MUIR (1838–1914), SCOTTISH-BORN NATURALIST

27 / THURSDAY

28 / FRIDAY

29 / SATURDAY

30 / SUNDAY

EXPLORE THE NATURAL WORLD

Though we often view nature as something separate from ourselves, we are, in fact, all part of it. This week, spend time alone outside. Lie down in the grass, contemplate the petals of a flower and watch the birds or the leaves rippling in the wind. Feel your links with nature resonate in you and make you feel more connected.

SEPTEMBER OVERVIEW

M	TU	W	TH	F	SA	SU
27	28	29	30	31	1	2
3	4	5	6	7	8	9
10	11	12	13	14	15	16
17	18	19	20	21	22	23
24	25	26	27	28	29	30

This month I am grateful for . . .

Reflections on CONNECTION

How did you bring more connections into your life this month?

What did it feel like to be more in touch with others and the world around you?

In what ways will you aim for deeper connections in the future?

OCTOBER

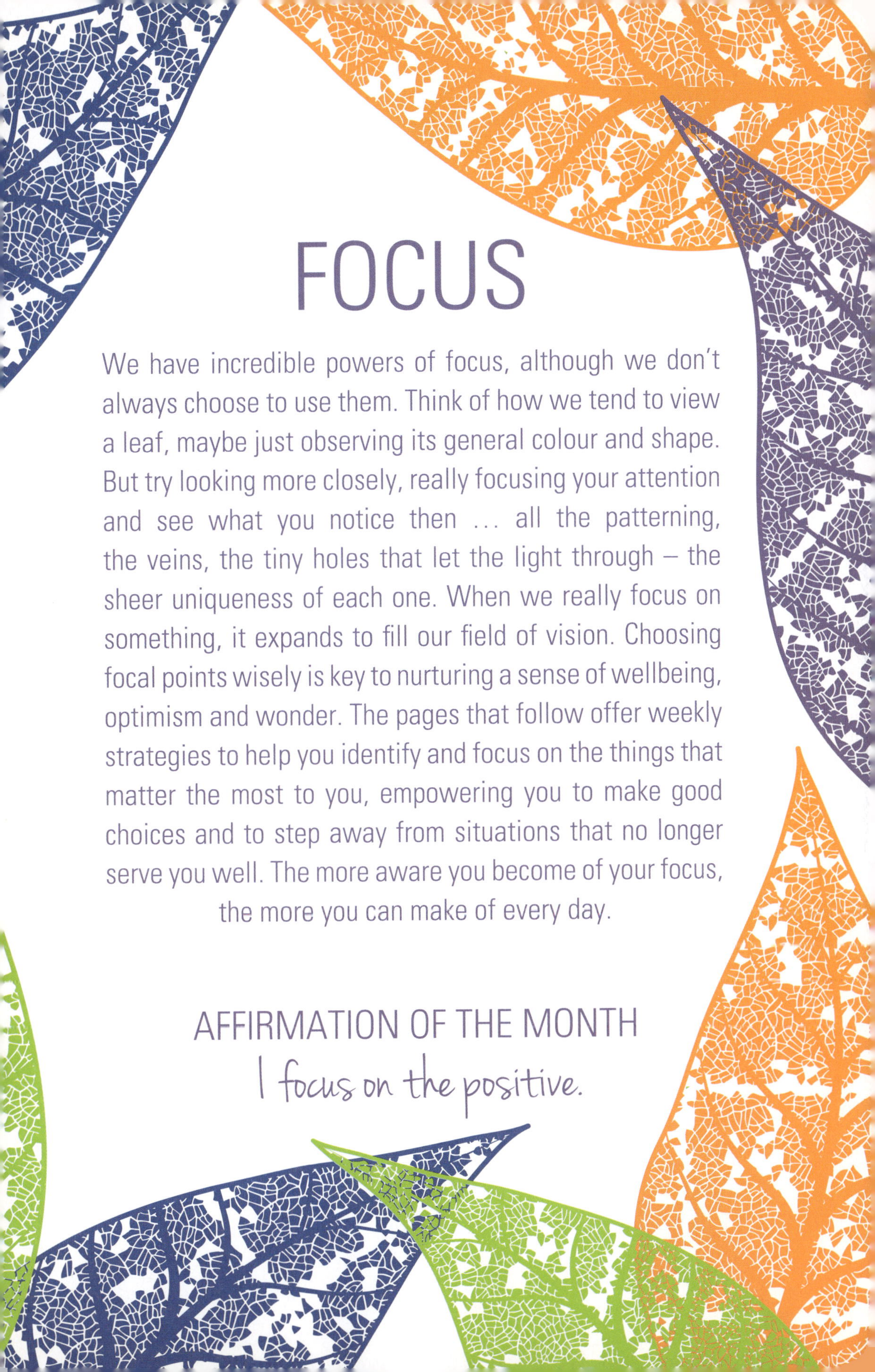

FOCUS

We have incredible powers of focus, although we don't always choose to use them. Think of how we tend to view a leaf, maybe just observing its general colour and shape. But try looking more closely, really focusing your attention and see what you notice then … all the patterning, the veins, the tiny holes that let the light through – the sheer uniqueness of each one. When we really focus on something, it expands to fill our field of vision. Choosing focal points wisely is key to nurturing a sense of wellbeing, optimism and wonder. The pages that follow offer weekly strategies to help you identify and focus on the things that matter the most to you, empowering you to make good choices and to step away from situations that no longer serve you well. The more aware you become of your focus, the more you can make of every day.

AFFIRMATION OF THE MONTH
I focus on the positive.

1 / MONDAY

Black History Month begins (UK)
Public holiday (ACT, NSW, QLD, SA)

2 / TUESDAY ☾

3 / WEDNESDAY

NOTES

ARISTOTLE ONASSIS (1906–1975), GREEK SHIPPING MAGNATE

4 / THURSDAY

5 / FRIDAY

6 / SATURDAY

7 / SUNDAY

LOOK FOR THE LIGHT

During challenging times, try to focus on what's going right. This week, keep a notebook with you and, when something goes wrong, note down one possible silver lining to the situation. You may not be able to change what went wrong, but finding something positive in the experience will help you shift your focus.

8 / MONDAY

Thanksgiving (CAN)
Columbus Day

9 / TUESDAY ●

10 / WEDNESDAY

NOTES

WILLIAM ARTHUR WARD (1921–1994), AMERICAN AUTHOR

11 / THURSDAY

12 / FRIDAY

13 / SATURDAY

14 / SUNDAY

SEEK OUT A SOLUTION

Try to solve problems instead of dismissing them as the fault of something or someone else. Note three problems (big or small) you're encountering at the moment. Then, write down one step you can take this week to move toward a solution for each issue. Think creatively! If you get stuck for ideas, ask a friend for insight.

15 / MONDAY

16 / TUESDAY ☽

17 / WEDNESDAY

NOTES

18 / THURSDAY

19 / FRIDAY

20 / SATURDAY

21 / SUNDAY

AVOID MULTI-TASKING

The thought of a lengthy to-do list can make us try to do too much at once, and we end up feeling overwhelmed and disheartened when nothing seems to get finished. This week, instead of multi-tasking, give your full attention to one job at a time until it is completed — and enjoy crossing each one off your list.

22 / MONDAY

Labour Day (NZ)

23 / TUESDAY ♏

24 / WEDNESDAY ○

NOTES

HENRY DAVID THOREAU (1817–1862), AMERICAN AUTHOR

25/ THURSDAY

26 / FRIDAY

27 / SATURDAY

28 / SUNDAY

British Summer Time ends

BE MEANINGFULLY OCCUPIED

Have you ever felt you've had a hectic week but achieved very little? Not this week! Make two lists: one of chores that don't really matter (cleaning that cupboard can wait); the other of activities with impact (visiting a lonely relative, for example). This week, focus on achieving as many items on the second list as possible.

OCTOBER OVERVIEW

M	TU	W	TH	F	SA	SU
1	2	3	4	5	6	7
8	9	10	11	12	13	14
15	16	17	18	19	20	21
22	23	24	25	26	27	28
29	30	31	1	2	3	4

This month I am grateful for . . .

____

____

____

____

____

____

Reflections on FOCUS

What did you find most helpful to focus more on this month?

What felt different when you chose only one thing to focus on?

What things, people or experiences will you focus on more in the months ahead?

NOVEMBER

COMPASSION

Compassion could be described as a special combination of empathy and altruism – the gentleness of a petal combined with the selflessness of the breeze that carries it. It means not just considering the feelings of others but also desiring to help alleviate any suffering on their part. As well as being a fantastic foundation for good friendship and a caring society, practising compassion also assists us as individuals to feel less stressed and more content in ourselves, allowing us to enjoy more meaningful, caring relationships that reflect compassion back into our own lives. And as we see the effects of being more gentle, empathetic and compassionate to other people, hopefully we will be encouraged to be kinder to ourselves, too. The focus this month is on showing compassion in all areas of your life – including in the way you treat yourself.

AFFIRMATION OF THE MONTH

I treat myself and others with compassion.

OCTOBER 29 – NOVEMBER 4.

compassion

29 / MONDAY

October Bank Holiday (ROI)

30 / TUESDAY

31 / WEDNESDAY ☾

Halloween
Samhain

NOTES

1 / THURSDAY

All Saints' Day

2 / FRIDAY

All Souls' Day

3 / SATURDAY

4 / SUNDAY

Daylight Saving Time ends
(CAN, USA)

LIVE EACH DAY WITH COMPASSION

Every day this week, practise one compassionate act. On Monday, say, take a pre-cooked meal to an elderly neighbour; on Tuesday offer practical help to a colleague who's overloaded with work; on Wednesday call a friend who's going through a hard time … Reflect on how each act enriches both the other person's life and your own.

NOVEMBER 5 – NOVEMBER 11

compassion

5 / MONDAY

6 / TUESDAY

7 / WEDNESDAY ●

Diwali

NOTES

8 / THURSDAY

9 / FRIDAY

10 / SATURDAY

11 / SUNDAY

Remembrance Sunday (UK)
Veterans Day (USA)
Remembrance Day (CAN)

BE KIND TO YOURSELF

Last week you showed compassion for others; this week, try to be kind to yourself. We all have moments of fragility and frustration. Be as gentle with yourself as you would be with a best friend: make your inner dialogue supportive and nurturing, seek peaceful acceptance and ask for help from others if you need it.

NOVEMBER 12 – NOVEMBER 18

compassion

12 / MONDAY

13 / TUESDAY

14 / WEDNESDAY

NOTES

15 / THURSDAY ☽

16 / FRIDAY

17 / SATURDAY

18 / SUNDAY

MAKE A DIFFERENCE IN THE WORLD

This week, instead of feeling helpless in the face of suffering, can you help support a communal relief effort? Perhaps you could donate money, goods or time to a charity, soup kitchen or clothes bank. Small, compassionate contributions add up to make a real difference.

NOVEMBER 19 – NOVEMBER 25

compassion

19 / MONDAY

20 / TUESDAY

Milad un-Nabi (birthday of
the Prophet Muhammed)
begins at sundown

21 / WEDNESDAY

World Hello Day

NOTES

> *"What I cannot love, I overlook."*
> ANAÏS NIN (1903–1977), FRENCH ESSAYIST

22 / THURSDAY ♐

Thanksgiving Day (USA)

23 / FRIDAY ○

24 / SATURDAY

25 / SUNDAY

Milad un-Nabi (Shia) (birthday of the Prophet Muhammed) begins at sundown

ACCEPT OTHERS' FLAWS

Is there someone in your life who bothers you? Invite him or her for coffee and in your own mind start anew. Set out to focus on the positive, perhaps opening with a compliment to set the tone. Try to see this person with compassionate eyes and go beyond the flaws. You may be surprised how your views change.

26 / MONDAY

27 / TUESDAY

28 / WEDNESDAY

NOTES

29 / THURSDAY

30 / FRIDAY ☾

St Andrew's Day

1 / SATURDAY

World AIDS Day

2 / SUNDAY

First Sunday of Advent
Hanukkah begins at sundown

REALLY *LISTEN*

Our concern for others often makes us want to cheer them up and offer good advice, but sometimes the truly compassionate response is simply to be there and listen. This week, try to listen (without offering advice) to people who are suffering, allowing them a space to work through their problems for themselves.

NOVEMBER OVERVIEW

M	TU	W	TH	F	SA	SU
29	30	31	1	2	3	4
5	6	7	8	9	10	11
12	13	14	15	16	17	18
19	20	21	22	23	24	25
26	27	28	29	30	1	2

This month I am grateful for . . .

Reflections on COMPASSION

In what ways did you cultivate more compassion in your life this month?

How does being especially compassionate toward others make you feel?

What will you do to show greater compassion to yourself and others in the future?

Don't miss out on next year's diary!
See the back page for details on how to order your copy for 2019.

DECEMBER

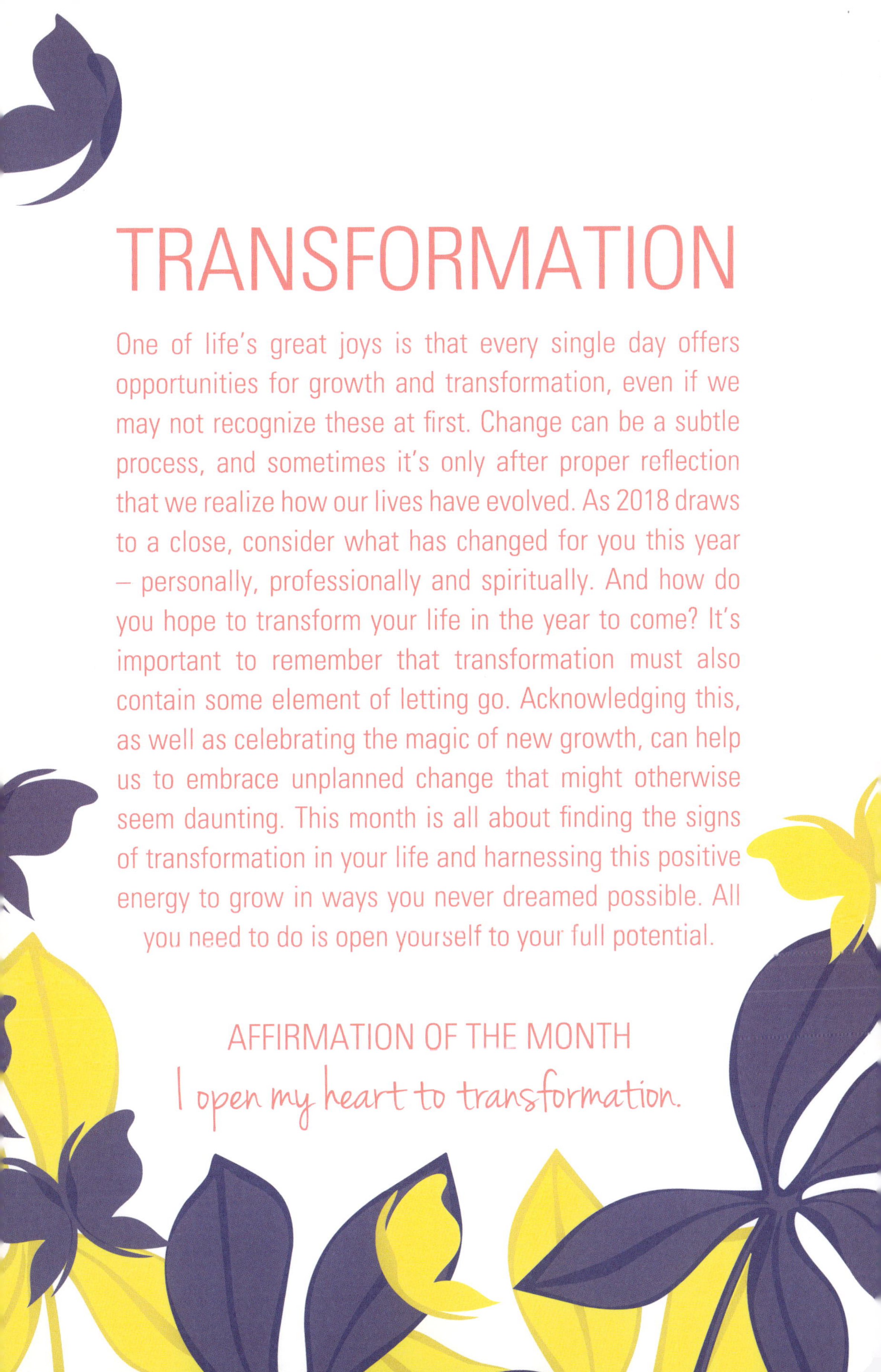

TRANSFORMATION

One of life's great joys is that every single day offers opportunities for growth and transformation, even if we may not recognize these at first. Change can be a subtle process, and sometimes it's only after proper reflection that we realize how our lives have evolved. As 2018 draws to a close, consider what has changed for you this year – personally, professionally and spiritually. And how do you hope to transform your life in the year to come? It's important to remember that transformation must also contain some element of letting go. Acknowledging this, as well as celebrating the magic of new growth, can help us to embrace unplanned change that might otherwise seem daunting. This month is all about finding the signs of transformation in your life and harnessing this positive energy to grow in ways you never dreamed possible. All you need to do is open yourself to your full potential.

AFFIRMATION OF THE MONTH

I open my heart to transformation.

DECEMBER 3 – DECEMBER 9

transformation

3 / MONDAY

4 / TUESDAY

5 / WEDNESDAY

NOTES

HENRY DAVID THOREAU (1817–1862), AMERICAN AUTHOR

6 / THURSDAY

7 / FRIDAY ●

8 / SATURDAY

Bodhi Day (Buddha's
Enlightenment) in some countries

9 / SUNDAY

IDENTIFY WHAT NEEDS TO CHANGE

This week, list all the things that hold you back
from enjoying life to the full – from small bad
habits to recurring negative attitudes. Consider
how much better life would be if you changed
these. Then write, "I can become _____" next to
each one. Hang the list somewhere you'll see it
every day to remind you of your potential.

DECEMBER 10 – DECEMBER 16

transformation

10 / MONDAY

11 / TUESDAY

12 / WEDNESDAY

NOTES

TONI CADE BAMBARA (1939–1995), AFRICAN-AMERICAN AUTHOR

13 / THURSDAY

14 / FRIDAY

15 / SATURDAY

16 / SUNDAY

WRITE IT OUT

Set aside two periods of 10–20 minutes this week. In the first, jot down a list of key things that have changed since the start of the year. Then, in the second session, freestyle everything you'd like to transform for the better in the coming year — and how you can make those changes. Don't edit; just let your ideas flow.

transformation

17 / MONDAY

18 / TUESDAY

19 / WEDNESDAY

NOTES

MOTHER TERESA (1910–1997), ALBANIAN-INDIAN MISSIONARY

20 / THURSDAY

21 / FRIDAY

Winter Solstice (UK, ROI, CAN, USA)
Summer Solstice (AUS, NZ)

22 / SATURDAY

23 / SUNDAY

MAKE WAVES WITH A SMALL ACTION

Do something small to create a ripple effect in your life and the lives of others this week. If, say, a loved one habitually does something annoying and you find yourself starting to snap as usual, take a deep breath and choose a different response. Your patience and kindness will mean everyone has a better day.

transformation

24 / MONDAY

Christmas Eve

25 / TUESDAY

Christmas Day

26 / WEDNESDAY

Boxing Day / St Stephen's Day
Kwanzaa begins

NOTES

27 / THURSDAY

28 / FRIDAY

29 / SATURDAY ☾

30 / SUNDAY

RELEASE WHAT YOU CANNOT UNDO

Although we can't alter the past or what other people do, we *can* control our reactions. Start transforming one aspect of your own life this week by saying out loud that you regret an episode from the past year (specify exactly what it is). Finish that statement with "… but I accept it as it is and let it go".

DECEMBER 31 – JANUARY 6

transformation

31 / MONDAY

New Year's Eve

1 / TUESDAY

New Year's Day
Kwanzaa ends

2/ WEDNESDAY

Public holiday (SCO, NZ)

NOTES

3 / THURSDAY

4 / FRIDAY

5 / SATURDAY

6 / SUNDAY ●

Epiphany

MAKE YOUR DREAM A REALITY

Earlier in the month you wrote about all the changes you would like to see in 2019. Explore one of these by creating a collage. On a large piece of paper, stick on words, cuttings, photos, drawings – anything that inspires and motivates you. If you can, set yourself a deadline for your goal and mark it in your diary for 2019.

DECEMBER OVERVIEW

M	TU	W	TH	F	SA	SU
26	27	28	29	30	1	2
3	4	5	6	7	8	9
10	11	12	13	14	15	16
17	18	19	20	21	22	23
24	25	26	27	28	29	30
31	1	2	3	4	5	6

This month I am grateful for . . .

Reflections on TRANSFORMATION

What does transformation mean to you now?

What positive transformations have taken place in your life this year?

What is your vision for the transformations you want to occur next year?

NOTE FROM THE AUTHOR

Hi! I'm Dani, the author and illustrator of the *Every Day Matters Diary*. This is one of my favourite projects every year, and I'm so grateful you chose it as the diary for you.

In 2009, I launched a website called PositivelyPresent.com and began dedicating my life to helping people around the world live with more positivity, awareness and self-esteem. I have since gone on to create a design company and a range of books that all seek to highlight the power of living positively in the present moment.

After working with Watkins Publishing on *The Positively Present Guide to Life*, I was delighted to have the opportunity in 2015 to develop the very first *Every Day Matters Diary*, as both author and illustrator. We've teamed up every year since to create a mindful, inspiring diary that helps make every single day of the year — of *your* year — matter!

If you like the themes in this year's diary, have a look at my series of "Effortless Inspiration" books. Packed with uplifting quotes, insightful reflections, thought-provoking activities and empowering affirmations, each one focuses on a different topic: *Living in the Moment*, *Gratitude*, *Compassion* and *Forgiveness*.

We very much hope you find this year's diary inspiring, motivating and above all enjoyable to use, and we can't wait to share the powerful themes we've chosen for 2019.

Wishing you a positive, peaceful and productive year!

dani

NOTES

DON'T MISS OUT ON NEXT YEAR'S DIARY!

To pre-order your 2019 *Every Day Matters* diaries from
September 2018 with FREE postage and packing,*
visit our website at watkinspublishing.com

Alternatively call our UK distributor on +44 (0)1206 255800.

*Free postage and packing for UK delivery addresses only. Offer limited to 3 books per order.

WATKINS

Sharing Wisdom Since
1893

Our books celebrate conscious, passionate, wise and happy living.
Be part of the community by visiting
watkinspublishing.com

WatkinsPublishing

WatkinsPublishingLtd

@watkinswisdom

+watkinspublishing1893